PIOUS & PROFESSIONAL
A GUIDE FOR MUSLIM WOMEN IN THE WORKFORCE

BY SOHAIR OMAR

Copyright © 2018 (AH 1439) by Sohair Omar

Design by Reyhana Ismail at www.reyoflightdesign.com
Cover image by bokehart/Shutterstock.com

All rights reserved. No part of this book may be reproduced in any language, stored in any retrieval system or transmitted in any form or by any means - electronic, mechanical, photocopying, recording or otherwise - without the express permission of the copyright owner. The views of the author do not necessarily reflect the views of the individuals appearing in this book.

To learn more about the Pious & Professional Project, send an e-mail to info@piousandprofessional.com.

First Edition

CONTENTS

Preface 03

Chapter 1: Introduction 05

Chapter 2: The Ultimate Goal: To Please Allah 06

Chapter 3: Halal v. Haram Work 08

Chapter 4: Dress Code & Personal Hygiene 10

Chapter 5: Everyday Communication 14

Chapter 6: Public Speaking & Meetings 17

Chapter 7: How To Interact With Your Male Colleagues 19

Chapter 8: Prayer Breaks & Holidays 21

Chapter 9: Family Planning & Maternity Leave 24

Chapter 10: Healthy Habits 27

Chapter 11: Giving Back 28

PREFACE

I begin with the Name of Allah, The Most Gracious, The Most Merciful.

Firstly, I thank Allah The All-Mighty, for inspiring me to write this book. Any good in it is from Allah, The All-Wise, and any mistakes are mine. I also thank my parents, Naeem Mahmood Omar and Amtul Rashid, and Overcoming Life's Obstacles Counseling for their support, Imam Abdullah Madyun for editing it, and Rey of Light Design for preparing it for publication.

CHAPTER 1
INTRODUCTION

Contrary to popular belief, Muslim women have participated in the workforce for centuries, dating back to Khadijah bint Khuwaylid, the first wife and follower of Prophet Muhammad (peace be upon him) and a successful merchant.

Some of us have the luxury of pursuing our careers while for others working is a matter of survival. Their right, as bestowed upon Muslim women in the Qur'an, to be "fed and clothed" is simply not being fulfilled.

"Men are the protectors and maintainers of women, because Allah has made one of them to excel the other, and because they spend [to support them] from their means. Therefore the righteous women are devoutly obedient [to Allah and to their husbands], and guard in the husband's absence what Allah orders them to guard (e.g., their chastity, their husband's property)...." Qur'an 4:34

No matter the case, once a Muslim woman enters the workforce, she will, without a doubt, face pressures to compromise her values for the sake of job security and/or career advancement (e.g., promotions, upward salary adjustments).

I'm here to tell her: Don't compromise. You can be pious and professional.

"And hold fast, all of you together, to the Rope of Allah, and be not divided among yourselves...." Qur'an 3:103

Let us together set the new professional standards for Muslim women.

CHAPTER 2
THE ULTIMATE GOAL: TO PLEASE ALLAH

As I type, I remind myself.

The ultimate goal in life is to please Allah, The All-Mighty.

"Allah has promised the believers - men and women - Gardens under which rivers flow to dwell therein forever, and beautiful mansions in Gardens of 'Aden (Eden Paradise). But the greatest bliss is the Good Pleasure of Allah. That is the supreme success." Qur'an 9:72

Don't be fooled. Society tells us to get a good job, to get rich, to buy a big house and a nice car, and to take expensive vacations. It defines success by material wealth and recognition by others. Some cultures even pressure us to become a doctor or to earn multiple degrees without any consideration of supply and demand of certain jobs.

"He who faces misfortunes with perseverance, Allah compensates him. He who acts only for fame and reputation, Allah disgraces him. He who shows patience and forbearance, Allah gives him a double reward." Prophet Muhammad (peace be upon him)

There's nothing wrong with being or trying to become wealthy but that's NOT the end goal.

"So when you have finished (your occupation), devote yourself for Allah's worship." Qur'an 94:7

Everything is wrong with it if it comes at the price of your faith (Iman). Always put Allah first - in every matter, even your career.

Turn down a promotion if it means that you'll be Director of Haram. Change careers if the industry that you're in does what Allah forbids and/or harms our community. It may be unpopular. It may not be financially beneficial. But it is pleasing to Allah and He is the best of providers.

Make tough decisions and sacrifice for the sake of Allah. (Perform Salat Al-Istikharah if you're unsure about something.)

That is success.

"But know by your Lord, they can have no faith until they make you (O Muhammad (peace be upon him)) judge in all disputes between them, and find in themselves no resistance against your decisions, and accept [them] with full submission." Qur'an 4:65

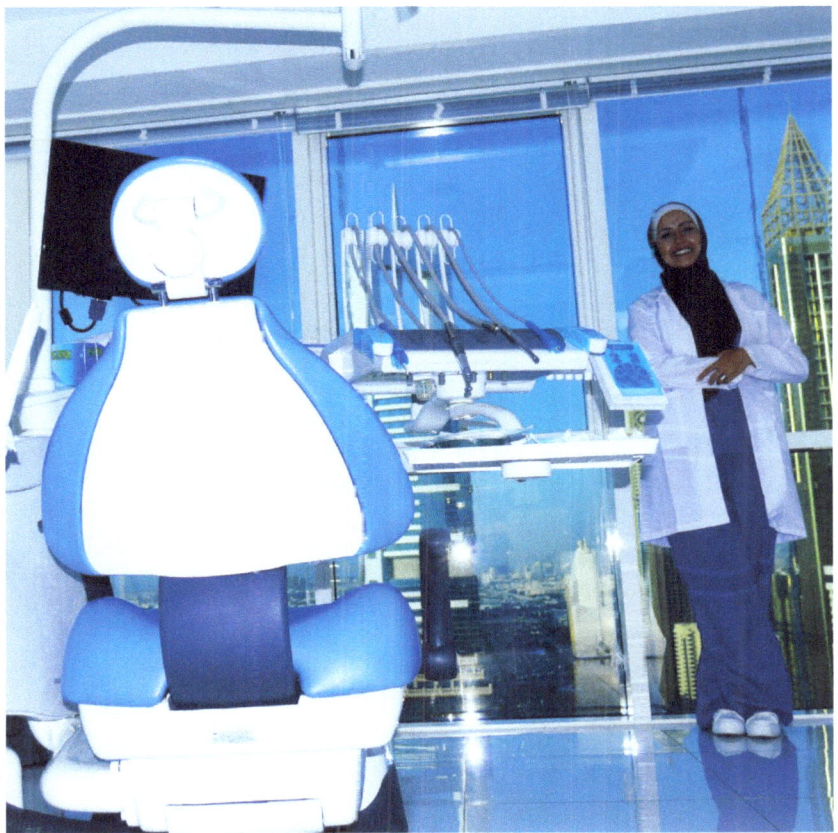

© Dr. Reem Alhasan

CHAPTER 3
HALAL V. HARAM WORK

Knowingly or unknowingly, many Muslims in the US participate in prohibited (Haram) economic activities - whether it's working at a bank that charges and collects interest (Riba), operating a convenient store or gas station that sells cigarettes and lottery (gambling), or working at or owning a restaurant that serves alcoholic beverages and/or pork. These examples are clear violations of the Qur'an and should NOT be followed.

"They ask you (O Muhammad (peace be upon him)) concerning alcoholic drink and gambling. Say: 'In them is a great sin, and benefits for men, but the sin of them is greater than their benefit.' And they ask you what they ought to spend. Say: 'That which is beyond your needs.' Thus Allah makes clear to you His Laws in order that you may give thought." Qur'an 2:219

"O you who believe! Be afraid of Allah and give up what remains from Riba (usury), if you are believers. And if you do not do it, then take a notice of war from Allah and His Messenger but if you repent, you shall have your capital sums. Deal not unjustly, and you shall not be dealt with unjustly." Qur'an 2:278-279

Generally, avoid working at, doing business with, and promoting companies and organizations that are involved in the following activities:

• Interest (interest-based banking and insurance; the production, sale or regulation of interest-bearing financial products)
• Gambling (including raffles)
• Alcohol and any other intoxicant
• Tobacco
• Pork and pork byproducts
• Pornography (and, obviously, prostitution)

- Homosexuality (It is NOT permissible in Islam no matter what the popular opinion is.)

Also, if your employer has too much debt, you may want to start thinking about an exit strategy.

It is wise to work in a profitable, growing industry so long as it is Halal. (Everything not mentioned above constitutes Halal work. You have many options!)

anythings/Shutterstock.com

CHAPTER 4
DRESS CODE & PERSONAL HYGIENE

The way Muslim women dress is a hotly debated topic among women, men and governments worldwide. The takeaway: You are powerful. The way you dress sends a powerful message.

"O Prophet! Tell your wives and your daughters and the women of the believers to draw their cloaks all over their bodies. That will be better, that they should be known [as free respectable women] so as not to be annoyed. And Allah is Ever Oft-Forgiving, Most Merciful." (Qur'an 33:59)

The overarching goal is to dress modestly and neatly.

Here are some dos and don'ts:

Always dress professionally. At minimum, own 3-5 formal outfits. No T-shirts. No jeans. No pictures and/or writings on clothes.

"Allah is beautiful and likes beauty. Putting on fine clothes is not pride." Prophet Muhammad (peace be upon him)

Full coverage of a woman's body except her face, hands and feet is standard in Islam. Headscarves should be wrapped neatly. (*Tip:* Rewrap your scarf every 1-3 hours. If you haven't mastered the art of wrapping a headscarf, watch tutorials by pros online.) If you wear a Niqab or Burka, right on! If you do not wear a headscarf, tie your hair up neatly.

"O Asma! When a girl attains her puberty, it is not proper that any organ of her body remains exposed save her face and palms." Prophet Muhammad (peace be upon him)

Strike a balance between fitted (not too fitted) and loose (not too loose) clothes. At minimum, the shapes of your body parts should not be visible.

Generally, wear more long dresses, long skirts and long coats and less pants and suits. The minimum length of shirts should be below the butt and "V" in front. Full sleeves only. (Three quarter sleeves are not full sleeves.)

"Allah sends curses on those men who take up female fashions and Allah curses such women who adopt a masculine style." Prophet Muhammad (peace be upon him)

Solid colors are recommended. Pastel colors, white and/or black - It's your choice! Avoid bright colors and busy prints. No see-through clothes.

"Simplicity in dress is one of the signs of faith in Allah." Prophet Muhammad (peace be upon him)

The same goes for shoes regarding color. Own 1-2 formal and comfortable shoes with low to no heels that do not make the "click, click" sound when walking. No holed or dirty socks or hosiery. No sneakers in professional settings.

Your personal hygiene is equally important.

"Cleanliness is half our faith (Iman)." Prophet Muhammad (peace be upon him)

Here's some general advice:

- Clean teeth and fresh breath are must-haves! Our Prophet (peace be upon him) recommended using Miswak (toothbrush) during every Wudu (ablution).
- No strong scents or odors.
- Keep your finger and toe nails clean and short at all times.
- If you wear makeup, wear light makeup, not heavy.
- If you wear jewelry, keep it to a minimum.

CHAPTER 5
EVERYDAY COMMUNICATION

You are a powerful symbol of Islam.

Always be conscious of and improve every aspect of your communications.

Men and women have a tendency of not taking women seriously, especially young women. Let them know from the first encounter that you mean business.

NONVERBAL
Develop and maintain a no non-sense attitude and calm, relaxed facial expressions. Maintain your composure at all times.

Have good posture (shoulders back, chin parallel to the floor and stomach pulled in). Develop confident sitting and standing positions. Walk confidently taking firm steps.

VERBAL
Develop an adult voice. It should be a balance between a soft, low voice and a loud, obnoxious voice.

"O wives of the Prophet! You are not like any other women. If you keep your duty (to Allah), then be not soft in speech, lest he in whose heart is a disease should be moved with desire, but speak in an honorable manner." Qur'an 33:32

Be assertive. Speak clearly. Speak with conviction. (If you don't believe in what you're saying, no one else will.)

CONTENT AND MEANINGFUL COMMUNICATION
Keep all commitments and promises or don't make them.

"Those who are faithfully true to their Amanat (all the duties which Allah has ordained, honesty, moral responsibility and trusts, and to their covenants. And those who strictly guard their Salawat. These are indeed the inheritors who shall inherit the Firdaus (Paradise). They shall dwell therein forever." Qur'an 23:8-11

"One who does not keep his word is not a man of faith." Prophet Muhammad (peace be upon him)

Be content and facts-driven. Do not disclose any personal information to anyone unless absolutely necessary.

Be prepared to answer basic questions about Islam. (Learn about Islam for yourself first. Use primary sources, Qur'an and Sunnah of Prophet Muhammad (peace be upon him).)

Learn the art of teaching, pedagogy. No matter what field you're in, you should know how to teach your colleagues and break concepts down or walk them through a process. (According to Al-Mustadrak, one fourth of our religion was narrated on the authority of A'ishah bint Abu Bakr.)

Always communicate formally and strategically (i.e., what to say, who to say it to, when to say it, how to say it (word choice, nonverbal communication) and what method of communication to use).

Be cordial, courteous and considerate at all times. Generously send meaningful thank you notes and cards.

Never gossip or backbite. If a person or group starts gossiping or backbiting, turn away.

"O you who believe! Avoid much suspicion; indeed some suspicions are sins. And spy not, neither backbite one another. Would one of you like to eat the flesh of his dead brother? You would hate it (so hate backbiting). And fear Allah. Verily, Allah is the One Who forgives and accepts repentance, Most Merciful." Qur'an 49:12

"Successful indeed are the believers ... those who turn away from Al-Laghw (dirty, false, evil vain talk, falsehood, and all that Allah has forbidden)." Qur'an 23:1-3

"Whoever spreads false news to make others laugh is liable to destruction."
Prophet Muhammad (peace be upon him)

Refrain from using common sayings and expressions without knowing their meaning and history. For example, "Jeez" is short for "Jesus" (peace be upon him).

"The tongue that is addicted to false expression is a bubbling spring of sins."
Prophet Muhammad (peace be upon him)

Be a perfectionist. Always double check your work for accuracy and completeness before sharing it with others.

Be punctual. Better yet, early. (If your meeting is at 10:00 am, be there at 9:45 am.)

Be responsive. Return phone calls and e-mail and text messages within 24 hours.

Lastly, mind your business.

"Part of the perfection of one's Islam is his leaving that which does not concern him."
Prophet Muhammad (peace be upon him)

gpointstudio/Shutterstock.com

CHAPTER 6
PUBLIC SPEAKING & MEETINGS

Polish your public speaking skills - no matter what field you're in.

Rehearsing makes perfect and comfortable. Join a public speaking group, such as Toastmasters International, if you can afford it. Practice speaking in front of a mirror regularly. Record yourself delivering a speech and watch it This helps a lot. Use your hands effectively while speaking. (*Tip:* Watch the pros on TV and online.)

Regarding content, get to the point. Don't make more than 3 to 5 points in one speech. Don't use unnecessary words or sounds (e.g., "like," "um," etc.). Storytelling is a plus.

Always begin your speeches with the Name of Allah. Acknowledge respected elders and distinguished members of the audience and greet them with peace. Do not shake hands with the opposite sex on stage. (Alternatively place your right hand over your heart and nod.)

The same goes for meetings. Always begin your meetings with the Name of Allah and greet meeting participants with peace.

Prepare and rehearse before meetings too. Specifically, list your desired outcomes. (*Tip:* Familiarize yourself with Robert's Rules of Order and learn how to facilitate a meeting professionally.)

Make decisions at meetings by consensus and consultation (Shura).

"And those who answer the Call of their Lord, and perform As-Salat, and who [conduct] their affairs by mutual consultation, and who spend of what We have bestowed on them."
Qur'an 42:38

If it's a gathering of Muslims, end your meetings by reciting Surat Al-Asr and a closing prayer. Prophet Muhammad (peace be upon him) used to say, when leaving a gathering: "Glory and praise be to You, O Allah. There is no god but You. I seek Your forgiveness and I repent to You."

These are priceless, must-have skills. Hone them.

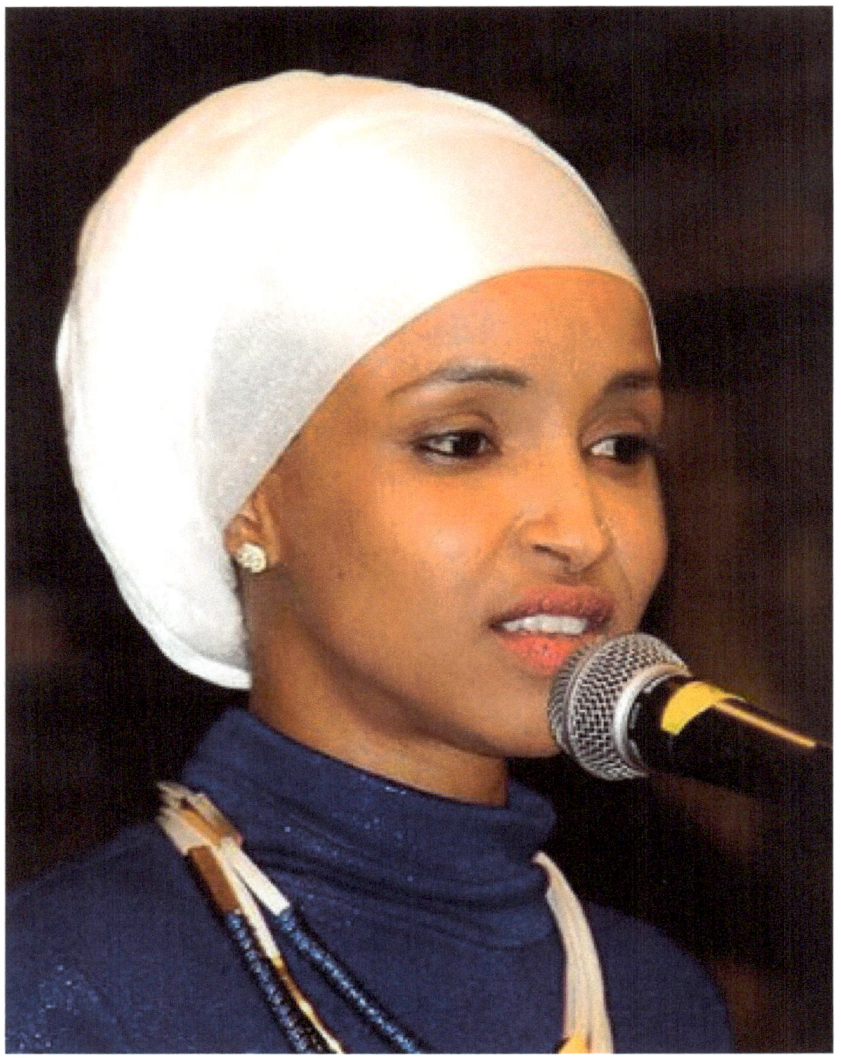

© Representative Ilhan Omar

CHAPTER 7
HOW TO INTERACT WITH YOUR MALE COLLEAGUES

Your male colleagues are most likely not Mahram.

"And tell the believing women to lower their gaze, and protect their private parts and not to show off their adornment except only that which is apparent, and to draw their veils all over Juyubihinna and not to reveal their adornment except to their husbands, or their fathers, or their husband's fathers, or their sons, or their husband's sons, or their brothers or their brother's sons, or their sister's sons, or their women, or the (female) slaves whom their right hands possess, or old male servants who lack vigor, or small children who have no sense of feminine sex. And let them not stamp their feet so as to reveal what they hide of their adornment. And all of you beg Allah to forgive you all, O believers, that you may be successful." Qur'an 24:31

Firstly, do not make physical contact with your male colleagues. No hugs. No handshakes. To greet them, place your right hand over your heart and say "Hello." If they try to hug you, put your hand on their chest and stop them. Then, say, "Sorry, I do not give hugs to men." If they try to shake your hand, politely decline and briefly explain why or say "I prefer not to shake hands with men." Don't give in. Your adherence to our code of conduct will make it easier for the next Muslim woman they encounter

Keep a distance. Never be in an office or room alone with a man. Look away if a man is in close proximity like in an elevator. Don't make prolonged or unnecessary eye contact with men. No winking.

Generally, reduce giggling and unnecessary smiling.

Keep it strictly business. Do not go on unnecessary outings, including lunches and dinners, with your male colleagues. Always decline invitations to happy hour.

Some men have a tendency to cut women off when they're speaking or talk over them. Learn how to do the same thing and do it sparingly when you have an important point to make.

If you're a victim of sexual harassment, which is all too common these days, immediately notify the men in your family and follow your company/organization and jurisdiction's sexual harassment complaint procedures. If you let him go, he'll do it to another woman or girl.

Not all men are sexual predators. You can learn a lot from them.

Take preventive measures and focus on your job.

bokehart/Shutterstock.com

CHAPTER 8
PRAYER BREAKS & HOLIDAYS

Prayer takes priority over work. Drop everything to pray on time.

"And those who strictly guard their Salawat. These are indeed the inheritors who shall inherit the Firdaus (Paradise). They shall dwell therein forever." Qur'an 23:9-11

"So woe unto those performers of Salat Those who delay their Salat (from their stated fixed times)." Qur'an 107:4-5

In the midst of meetings, I would often say to my colleagues, "Please excuse me. I have to take a prayer break."

If your employer does not have a chapel or a space for meditation, which is becoming common among leading companies, find an empty room to pray in.

Notify your employer - specifically your supervisor and/or HR department - of your obligation to pray in advance. (Here's what you can say: "Muslims have to pray five times a day - before sunrise, around noon, mid-afternoon, at sunset and at night. We have to stop everything that we're doing and take five minutes to praise and thank God. I may use my breaks to pray. Thank you for understanding.") You may also attend Jum'ah (Friday congregational prayer) at the nearest Masjid during an extended lunch break or another arrangement with your employer so long as no work is missed.

Do not feel embarrassed to perform Wudu (ablution) at work. If someone is looking at you, just say "I'm washing before praying. Please don't mind." Be sure to wipe the sink and floor dry when you're done.

© Fatimah Aulaqi

Take Eid off from work - both of them - and explain our holidays to your employer.

For example, say:

"I am requesting [DATE] off to observe a religious holiday, Eid Al-Fitr, which marks the end of Ramadan, a holy month during which Muslims fast and empathize with the poor."

"I am requesting [DATE] off to observe a religious holiday, Eid Al-Adha, which commemorates Prophet Abraham's willingness to sacrifice his son in obedience to God."

Unless Muslims stop working and sending their kids to school on Eid, it will not be recognized widely. Do your part.

Regarding Hajj (pilgrimage to Mecca), if you can afford it, use your vacation time and go!

"... And Hajj to the House (Ka'bah) is a duty that humankind owes to Allah, those who can afford the expenses; and whoever disbelieves, then Allah stands not in need of any of the 'Alamin." Qur'an 3:97

CHAPTER 9
FAMILY PLANNING & MATERNITY LEAVE

First and foremost, marry a man who recognizes your talent and potential and is committed to supporting your personal and professional growth. It makes a BIG difference.

Time your pregnancies according to your career trajectory. But don't wait too long. Physical recovery from childbirth is slower in your 30s and 40s than it is in your 20s. Plus, have your children while your parents and grandparents are alive. You WILL need their support (again). It literally takes a village to raise a child. (*Note*: Pregnancy and childbirth are not always easy. Miscarriages, still births and a number of medical complications are realities for many women. Be mentally prepared for Allah's tests.)

Nurse your baby for two whole years. It's the best food for your baby! (*Warning*: Breastfeeding is not easy. Seek assistance, if you need it.)

"The mothers shall give suck to their children for two whole years, for those who desire to complete the term of suckling, but the father of the child shall bear the cost of the mother's food and clothing on a reasonable basis. No person shall have a burden laid on him greater than he can bear. No mother shall be treated unfairly on account of her child, nor father on account of his child. And on the heir is incumbent the like of that. If they both decide on weaning, by mutual consent, and after due consultation, there is no sin on them. And if you decide on a foster suckling-mother for your children, there is no sin on you, provided you pay [the foster suckling-mother] what you agreed [to give her] on reasonable basis. And fear Allah and know that Allah is All-Seer of what you do." Qur'an 2:233

For maternity leave, 1-2 years is recommended. If that is not an option for you, take 6 months off at minimum. Your child needs YOU. (The current US standard of 6 weeks to 3 months is unnatural.) Plan accordingly.

Becoming a mother is a blessing but it is also hard.

"And We have enjoined on man [to be dutiful and good] to his parents. His mother bore him in weakness and hardship upon weakness and hardship, and his weaning is in two years - give thanks to Me and to your parents. Unto Me is the final destination."
Qur'an 31:14

Postpartum depression is real.

Be prepared to responsibly lose your pregnancy weight (without negatively affecting your milk supply) and to rebuild your self-confidence.

Maternity leave may result in lower pay, lesser promotions compared to your male counterparts. If you're a victim of pay inequality and your ego can't take it, have a plan B and a plan C and get creative! Use your time off to redefine yourself, as a sabbatical, or to change careers. That decision is for you to make strategically.

Zurijeta/Shutterstock.com

CHAPTER 10
HEALTHY HABITS

Adopting healthy habits will significantly improve your performance.

Get 8-9 hours of sleep per night at minimum.

Go to bed early and wake up early. (For many people, the most productive hours of the day are in the morning.) According to A'ishah bint Abu Bakr, Prophet Muhammad (peace be upon him) would not sleep before Salat Al-'Isha and he would not stay up after it.

Exercise regularly and moderately. Follow a physical fitness program/workout routine that suits you (e.g., yoga, walking, etc.).

Eat wholesome, nutritious food including fresh fruits and vegetables. Pack your own Halal lunch and healthy snacks (e.g., fruits and nuts) for work.

Cut down on meat and your portions generally.

"The son of Adam cannot fill a vessel worse than his stomach, for it is enough for him to take a few bites to straighten his back. If he must, then he may fill it one-third with food, one-third with drink, and one-third with breath." Prophet Muhammad (peace be upon him)

Lastly, beware of burnout. Do not overbook yourself. Manage your schedule and commitments responsibly. It's okay - and sometimes better - to say no.

These tips alone will make you feel and look better.

Take care of yourself. You're worth it!

CHAPTER 11
GIVING BACK

Live to give - your time, professional expertise, sincere advice and/or seed money.

Whenever possible, support other Muslim women.

"All Muslims are like the bricks of a building that support each other." Prophet Muhammad (peace be upon him)

Mentoring a young Muslim woman is one of the most high-impact contributions that you can make. (*Tip:* Set expectations and guidelines for your relationship with your mentee in the beginning. Check in or meet face-to-face with her at least once a month and make yourself available to her via phone and/or e-mail for time-sensitive matters. Always keep Allah first in your conversations.)

Other ways to help a young Muslim woman include:

• Freely give her workplace tips and career advice;
• Hire her based on merit;
• Fund her invention(s) and/or technical education;
• Formally introduce her to key people in your network; and
• Always encourage and empower her.

Let's face it. The odds are stacked against us. We must uplift one another. We must invest in one another.

This book is my sincere advice to you.

www.ingramcontent.com/pod-product-compliance
Lightning Source LLC
Chambersburg PA
CBHW040301220526
45473CB00002B/547